TheMUSICofLOVE

PRESENTS

The Practical Guide to
WEDDING MUSIC

Everything you need to know to find and negotiate
with wedding musicians for perfect music at a great price.

Written & Compiled by
John R. Schneider

Edited by
Karen Oliver

Endorsed by

CONTENTS OF GUIDE:

Introduction to Guide - 1

As a musician who plays the "music of love" at weddings and receptions — and as someone who has a deep appreciation for timeless love songs and poetry — I wanted to share with you my practical and business experience as a musician who has been interviewed innumerable times by brides, grooms and wedding planners to help them determine if I'm the right musician at the right price for their event.

It may be obvious, but the right musician playing the perfect music can make such a difference in the way you experience and remember your special day. However, finding musicians may be challenging because there is a seemingly endless supply of us. Just search on the Internet for "wedding musician" and you'll see what I mean. Also, it may be difficult to distinguish those musicians who will most likely meet your expectations from those who won't.

Finally, negotiating with musicians isn't something most people do every day, so it can be confusing to know how much you'll need to spend. I'll provide you with some insight on how musicians establish their fees, why there's such a diverse range of rates, and now to negotiate successfully for the rate your desire to pay.

I'm grateful to many of the wedding planners who have shared their own experiences with me over the years. Equally important has been the great feedback received from brides and grooms who also helped me learn a good deal about what it takes to have a successful wedding and reception.

I hope this guide is helpful to you as you plan your wedding and reception. In addition, you'll find numerous web sites on the Internet which provide a plethora of insight and information. If you have unanswered questions, please don't hesitate to contact me directly. You may also visit my website — TheMUSICofLOVE.com — for additional information.

My special thanks to Karen Oliver who contributed and edited content.

My very best wishes to you!

John Schneider
TheMUSICofLOVE.com

2 - WEDDING FACTS TODAY

Here's the latest information on wedding expenses, music, rings and honeymoon destinations:

- According to a poll of brides and grooms taken by WeddingZone.net, the most important aspect of the wedding reception is MUSIC:

    46% - Music & Entertainment
    25% - Food
    14% - Location & Venue
     6% - Photography & Videography
     5% - Flowers & Decorations

- $19 billion is spent buying presents at wedding gift registries.

- 19% of all engagements occur in December.

- The average engagement lasts 13 months.

- The traditional wedding costs $22,000 with 200 guests.

- The average second wedding costs $12,000, but the couples spend nearly double what first-time couples do on their honeymoons.

- The average ring costs $2,000.

- 74% of all engaged couples receive a diamond engagement ring. 60% of people are not involved in selecting their engagement ring, while 3% actually choose it themselves.

- The wedding ring has traditionally been worn on the third finger of the left hand because it was believed that a vein in this finger ran directly to the heart. The third finger of the left hand has become the customary wedding-ring finger for all English-speaking cultures.

- 62% of weddings have a flower person, while 56% have a ring bearer.

- 80% of couples plan formal or traditional weddings.

- In 2000, the average engaged couple was between 24 and 28 years old.

- Only 4% of couples asked for the parents' approval for their partners' hand in marriage.

- 20% of wedding proposals are made on one knee.

- 6% of couples proposed over the phone.

- Average Honeymoon cost is $3,500 for 7 Nights

- Top Honeymoon Destinations:
    Caribbean 31%
    Hawaii 15%
    Mexico 15%

Sources: Wedding Musician Association, Association of Bridal Consultants, Condé Nast Bridal Group, Mediapost.com, National Bridal Service, National Center for Health Statistics, Greeting Card Association, National Association of Wedding Ministers, and SimplyBeautifulWeddingPlanning.com.

4 - EVENTS & MUSIC FOR WEDDING CEREMONY

Wedding ceremonies come in all varieties, but here's one example of how events may be ordered in a traditional wedding ceremony:

PRELUDE MUSIC

Music of the Prelude is played 30 to 45 minutes before the ceremony and helps to set the mood for the wedding. For example, if the wedding is in a church, then the music of a quiet piano or acoustic guitar will allow guests an opportunity to pray, reflect or engage in quiet conversation.

WEDDING PROCESSIONALS

The wedding ceremony begins with the entrance of the bridal party. Normally, the ushers lead the procession, followed by the bridesmaids, maid/matron of honor, the ring bearer, and then the flower girl. The music selection should begin softly with the volume increasing gradually until it's time for the bride's entrance. Since the bride's entrance is the most important part of the processional, there should be a noticeable increase in volume when it's time for her to enter. Traditional music may include:

Canon in D – Johann Pachelbel
Here Comes the Bride (Bridal Chorus) – Wagner
Jesu, Joy of Man's Desiring – Bach
Trumpet Voluntary – Jeremiah Clarke
Canon in F – The O'Neill Brothers
Ode to Joy – Beethoven
Hymne – Vangelis
Spring (from Four Seasons) – Antonio Vivaldi
Reminiscent Joy – The O'Neill Brothers
Edelweiss – Richard Rodgers
Ballade Pour Adeline – Richard Clayderman
Ashokan Farewell – Jay

WELCOME AND ADDRESS

The Welcome is delivered by the Officiant and includes personal details about the couple.

READINGS

Very often, two readings are selected. The wedding couple normally selects the readers who are usually members of the wedding party, close friends or family members. Readers should receive copies of their readings in advance.

VOCALIST & MUSICAL INTERLUDE

This is an optional time for a vocalist or short musical interlude.

INTRODUCTION TO THE VOWS

The Officiant explains the significance and meaning of the wedding vows.

EXCHANGE OF VOWS

The couple reads or speaks their written vows or repeats the vows delivered by the Officiant.

INTRODUCTION TO THE RINGS

The Officiant explains the importance and symbolism of the wedding rings.

EXCHANGE OF THE RINGS

The couple may speak their own words when exchanging rings, or repeat what the Officiant says.

UNITY CANDLE, WINE CEREMONY

The couple may choose to light a unity candle or have some other ceremony during a short musical interlude.

PRONOUNCEMENT

By the Officiant.

BLESSING AND CLOSING WORDS

By the Officiant

WEDDING RECESSIONALS

At the end of the ceremony, the bride and groom are announced as man and wife and exit together followed by the individuals in the wedding party. Music should be very upbeat and may include the following selections:

Wedding March – Felix Mendelssohn
Jesu, Joy of Man's Desiring – Bach
Canon in F – The O'Neill Brothers
Ode to Joy – Beethoven
Finale (from Water Music) – G.F. Handel
Rondeau – Mouret
Trumpet Tune – Henry Purcell

POSTLUDE

Music for the Postlude should begin after the Recessional and is played until all of the guests have been through the receiving line.

6 - EVENTS & MUSIC FOR WEDDING RECEPTION

1. Arrival of Guests: *Soft Piano Music*

It's always nice to have soft music playing in the reception area while drinks and light refreshments are served to guests arriving before the wedding party. Your Master of Ceremonies can make some announcements about when the wedding party is expected to arrive and then make sure everyone is seated or positioned correctly for the grand entrance.

2. Announcing Wedding Party: *Upbeat & Celebratory Instrumental Music*

Your MC will announce the wedding party after making sure that all guests are correctly positioned. The wedding party should be lined up in order of appearance outside the entrance to the reception area. The traditional order is the groom's parents, bride's parents, flower girl and ring bearer, bridesmaids escorted by ushers, maid of honor escorted by best man, and finally the bride & groom.

3. Positioning of Wedding Party & Group Photograph: *Music Continued*

4. Seating of Wedding Party: *Music Continued*

Your MC welcomes everyone once again as the wedding party is seated.

5. Champagne Toast

The toast should be done before the meal when all of your guests are seated. Normally, the first toast is made by the best man and may be followed by toasts from the maid of honor, friends, relatives, or even by the bride and groom. Very often, however, toasts by others can be made after dinner and during the dance. Your MC will get everyone's attention and introduce the best man.

6. The Blessing

Your MC will ask everyone to be seated and will introduce whoever will say the blessing.

7. Instructions for the Meal

Your MC (or the banquet manager) will provide any instructions for the meal.

8. Serving the Meal: *Soft Piano Music*

The bride, groom and wedding party are the first to be served. Soft piano music plays in the background during dinner.

9. Cutting the Cake: *Instrumental Music*

After the meal, the bride and groom cut the wedding cake together, hand-over-hand, and feed each other the first piece. Then the rest of the cake is cut and served to the guests. Another option is to cut the cake and serve it later in the evening.

10. Additional Toasts & Testimonials
While the cake is being cut and served, other members of the wedding party or other guests may wish to make toasts or short testimonials.

11. First Dance of Bride & Groom: *Personal Music Selection*
After everyone has eaten their cake, the first dance of the bride and groom marks their first dance as husband and wife. Depending upon the number of guests, the MC could invite everyone to stand outside of the dance floor to surround the bride and groom with a show of love and support.

12. Father & Bride Dance: *Personal Music Selection*

13. Mother & Groom Dance: *Personal Music Selection*

14. Dance of Entire Wedding Party: *Personal Music Selection*
The groom may wish to dance with his mother-in-law while the bride dances with her father-in-law. You may wish to skip this step and invite everyone to dance if the number of guests is small.

15. Welcome by Bride & Groom (Optional)
You may both step up to the microphone and welcome any special family members, say thank you and welcome everyone. You can also invite everyone to the dance floor.

16. Everyone Dances
Your MC invites everyone to the dance floor to dance.

17. Bouquet & Garter Toss: *Optional Music*
The bride tosses her bouquet to a group of single women and the groom removes the bride's garter and tosses it to a group of single men. Sometimes, these events are done before dinner. You may wish to skip this tradition if you have a small number of guests.

18. Bride & Groom's Last Dance: *Personal Music Selection*
If the bride and groom plan to leave before the end of the reception, this is their last dance together before departing the reception.

19. Last Dance of the Evening
The MC will make an announcement when it's getting near to the end of the reception and will announce the last dance. The MC should also thank any family members who are still at the reception.

8 – TOP LOVE SONGS

All the music of life seems to be like a bell that is ringing for me.

There are thousands of great love songs, but here are just a few to consider:

SONG	YEAR	ARTIST
All The Way	1957	Frank Sinatra
All I Really Wanna Do	1964	Bob Dylan
All You Need Is Love	1964	The Beatles
Almost Like Being In Love	1961	Judy Garland
Always On My Mind	1982	Willie Nelson
All My Loving	1963	The Beatles
Alone	1987	Heart
Always On My Mind	1982	Willie Nelson
Always	1987	Atlantic Starr
And I Love Her	1964	The Beatles
Baby, I Love Your Way	1976	Peter Frampton
Because You Loved Me	1996	Celine Dion
Best Of My Love	1977	The Emotions
Breathe	1999	Faith Hill
Bridge Over Troubled Water	1970	Simon & Garfunkel
Building A Mystery	1997	Sarah McLachlan
By Your Side	2000	Sade
Can't Help Falling In Love With You	1961	Elvis Presley
Can You Feel The Love Tonight?	1994	Elton John
Can't Take My Eyes Off Of You	1967	Frankie Valli
Cherish	1967	The Association
Close To You	1970	The Carpenters
Crazy For You	1987	Madonna

SONG	YEAR	ARTIST
Don't Speak	1995	No Doubt
Embraceable You	1943	Judy Garland
Endless Love	1981	Diana Ross & Lionel Richie
Eternal Flame	1988	The Bangles
Evergreen	1976	Barbra Streisand
Every Little Thing She Does Is Magic	1981	The Police
Everything I Do, I Do It For You	1991	Bryan Adams
Faint of Heart	2006	Vince Gill
Feelings	1975	Morris Albert
First Time Ever I Saw Your Face	1972	Roberta Flack
Fly Me To The Moon	1964	Frank Sinatra
For Once In My Life	1968	Stevie Wonder
Girl	1965	The Beatles
Groovy Kind Of Love	1965	The Mindbenders
Groovin'	1967	The Young Rascals
Happy Together	1967	The Turtles
Have I Told You Lately?	1993	Rod Stewart
Here And Now	1989	Luther Vandross
Here Comes The Sun	1969	The Beatles
Here, There And Everywhere	1966	The Beatles
How Deep Is Your Love	1978	The Bee Gees
How Do I Live	1997	LeAnn Rimes
I Believe	1965	The Letterman
I Could Have Danced All Night	1964	Julie Andrews
I Don't Want To Miss A Thing	2002	Aerosmith
I Feel For You	1984	Chaka Khan
I Got You Babe	1965	Sonny & Cher
I Just Want To Be Your Everything	1977	Andy Gibb
I Need Love	1987	LL Cool J
I Want To Hold Your Hand	1964	The Beatles
I Will Always Love You	1992	Whitney Houston
I Will	1968	The Beatles
I Would Die 4 U	1984	Prince
I'd Do Anything For Love	1993	Meat Loaf
If	1971	Bread
If I Fell	1964	The Beatles
If I Were A Carpenter	1966	Bobby Darin
I'll Be There For You	1989	Bon Jovi

SONG	YEAR	ARTIST
I'll Follow The Sun	1964	The Beatles
I'll Make Love To You	1994	Boyz II Men
I'll Stand By You	1994	The Pretenders
I'm A Believer	1966	The Monkees
In My Life	1965	The Beatles
It Must Have Been Love	1986	Roxette
It's Only Love	1977	The Beatles
Just The Two Of Us	1981	Bill Withers
Just The Way You Are	1977	Billy Joel
Kind Of A Hush	1967	Peter Noone
Letter, The	1967	The Boxtops
Let's Get It On	1973	Marvin Gaye
Let's Stay Together	1972	Al Green
Love Is A Many Splendored Thing	1955	The Four Aces
Love Is All Around	1966	The Troggs
Love Me Tender	1956	Elvis Presley
Love To Love You Baby	1976	Donna Summer
Love Will Keep Us Together	1975	Captain & Tennille
Maybe I'm Amazed	1970	Paul McCartney
Melt With You	1983	Modern English
More Than A Feeling	1976	Boston
More Than Words	1990	Extreme
My Funny Valentine	1955	Frank Sinatra
My Girl	1964	Smokey Robinson
My Heart Will Go On	1997	Celine Dion
Never My Love	1967	The Association
Never Tear Us Apart	1988	INXS
Nobody Wants To Be Lonely	2000	Ricky Martin
Nothing Compares 2 U	1990	Sinead O'Connor
Open Arms	1982	Journey
P.S. I Love You	1964	The Beatles
Romeo and Juliet	1981	Dire Straits
Rose, The	1980	Bette Midler
Save The Best For Last	1991	Vanessa Williams
Secret Garden	1995	Bruce Springsteen
She's Got A Way	1971	Billy Joel

SONG	YEAR	ARTIST
Stand By Me	1961	Ben E. King
Sunny	1963	Bobby Hebb
Stop To Love	1986	Luther Vandross
Something	1969	The Beatles
Sometimes When We Touch	1977	Dan Hill
Somewhere Over The Rainbow	1939	Judy Garland
Tell Me What You See	1965	The Beatles
Thank You	1999	Dido
That's The Way Love Goes	1993	Janet Jackson
This Boy	1964	The Beatles
This I Promise You	2000	NSYNC
Three Times A Lady	1978	The Commodores
Til There Was You	1963	The Beatles
Time After Time	1984	Cyndi Lauper
To Love Somebody	1967	The Bee Gees
Unchained Melody	1965	The Righteous Brothers
Unforgettable	1991	Natalie Cole f/ Nat King Cole
We Belong	1985	Pat Benatar
We've Only Just Begun	1970	The Carpenters
What A Wonderful World	1967	Louis Armstrong
When A Man Loves A Woman	1966	Percy Sledge
Wicked Game	1989	Chris Isaak
Wild Thing	1966	The Troggs
Woman	1981	John Lennon
Wonderful Tonight	1978	Eric Clapton
Words Of Love	1964	The Beatles
You Are So Beautiful	1975	Joe Cocker
You Are The Sunshine Of My Life	1973	Stevie Wonder
Your Song	1971	Elton John
You're In My Heart	1978	Rod Stewart
You're Still The One	1997	Shania Twain
You're The First, Last, My Everything	1975	Barry White
You're The One That I Want	1978	John Travolta

"If music be the food of love, play on."
William Shakespeare

12 - TYPES OF WEDDING MUSICIANS

What type of musician do you need?

Typically, wedding music could simply be pre-recorded selections from your collection of CDs. You could also decide to use a variety of musicians for the different parts of your wedding which require a different mood or sounds. Or, in some cases, you may be able to hire one musician to do it all. Above all else, make certain your musician is a member of a professional organization, such as the Wedding Musician Association. Here are types of musicians and their typical cost for two hours of music:

Classical Pianist	$300 - $400
Organist	$200 - $300
One-Man Band	$200 - $3,500
DeeJay	$100 - $3,000
Rock Band	$1,000 - $8,000
Orchestra	$2,000 - $10,000
String Quartet	$1,000 - $2,500
Violinist	$300 - $1,000
Flautist	$100 - $500
Acoustic Guitarist	$100 - $300
Vocalist	$100 - $500
Harpist	$100 - 500

Gigmasters.com says the most popular category of musicians for weddings and receptions is the "One Man Band."

How many musicians do you need?

It's not always easy to find <u>one</u> musician to play during every part of your wedding. For example, while a classical pianist may play during the wedding ceremony, a guitarist may play during the reception while a rock band may be setting up to play during the dance party. And if the dance party is in another location, it may be even more challenging. Usually, every musician will set up a sound system wherever they play, so it's not always possible for one individual to do it all – but it's not impossible either.

If you're trying to be cost-effective, look for a musician who can do it all. For example, a musician could play pre-recorded traditional music for your wedding ceremony, then play a quiet, but upbeat guitar during the reception and still play high-energy dance music during the party. You have a number of options, so make certain you explore them all.

TIPS FOR FINDING THE RIGHT MUSICIAN - 13

Whether your affair is grand or intimate, the right live music will be an important ingredient to making it successful. So, here are five suggestions for making it happen.

Don't start with a budget for music. Instead, envision the kind of wedding, ceremony and celebration you want to experience -- not what your guests or family want, but what you want. Forget about the cost for now. Believe me, if your vision is strong enough and you're creative enough, you will find a band or orchestra or guitar player or pianist within your budget. The supply of musicians far outweighs the demand. But if you wait until the last minute, you won't have time to shop around.

One size may not fit all. The musician you hire for the ceremony may be different than the musician for the reception. You could save a little money by negotiating with a band that can "break apart" to provide a pianist or acoustic guitar player for the ceremony and then joins back together for the reception and party. Another plus is when the front-person of the band can also be the Master of Ceremonies. If you get really lucky, you may even find a musician willing to write original music just for you. Be careful that you're not asking one musical group to do too much.

Seek an agreement. Make certain the live musician(s) you select can provide you with a written agreement – even an e-mail message – confirming their price, services and length of performance. It's also best if the musicians belong to a professional organization which sets forth principles to guide musicians' behavior during their performance. For example, the Wedding Musician Association publishes Principles of Performance which states musicians should not set up or break down their equipment while guests are still in attendance. Other principles include guidelines about wedding protocol, safety, and ethical billing procedures.

Stick to your guns. Even though musicians may have a lot of great ideas for music, you are the one in charge of your own vision. Certainly, they can influence you with their experience and you should listen to their ideas. But this is your time, your life, and your vision. Try to figure out -- in advance – all of the specific songs you want and then ask for samples so you can hear the music before the big day. Believe it or not, many musicians are happy to plan with you and some will even attend the rehearsal – and you should let them. In fact, don't forget that many couples have live music for their wedding rehearsal reception.

Ask for help, early. Just as it takes some people some time to find the right partner to share their life, it could take a little time to select the right musician and the most appropriate music. Don't be afraid to ask for help. Share your vision of music with a friend and turn them loose, but don't let them make decisions without you. In the end, you'll be glad you didn't wait until the last minute.

14 - QUESTIONS TO ASK WEDDING MUSICIANS

- Will you provide professional consultation regarding music?

- Will you listen to what I want to do?

- Will you allow us to select the music?

- Do you understand the components and protocol of weddings?

- Do you have the appropriate demeanor to be part of our event?

- Are you a Member of the Wedding Musician Association?

- Do you have references?

- Will you take reasonable 5-10 minute breaks between sets?

- Will you provide pre-recorded music when taking a break?

- Will you be available to meet with the wedding planner?

- Will you attend our wedding rehearsal?

- Will you provide sound samples or video?

- Can you play music in any venue, inside or outside?

- Will you allow us to see you play publicly?

- Will you provide a video of the dance party?

- Will you offer to learn new songs we'd like to hear?

- Do you understand how to play for different age groups?

- Are you "kid-friendly?"

- Will you let our guests play or sing along? If so, will you provide a microphone for guests?

- Will you make announcements & introduce the wedding party?

- Will you provide a clear, written agreement of what you'll offer?

- Will you offer fair and flexible prices for services?

- Can you play pre-recorded wedding music, when desired?

- Can you provide lighting for our event?

- Do you provide everything necessary, including lights and sound system?

Visit WeddingMusicianAssociation.org

NEGOTIATING RATES WITH WEDDING MUSICIANS - 15

How much is that piano-playing doggy in the window? Yes, the one with the waggley tail! The real answer is: How much are you willing to pay?

Demand and supply is the name of the game in the wedding music business. For example, everyone knows that — compared to a live band -- DeeJays are less expensive. Generally, there are two reasons why. First, DeeJays don't split their fee with anyone. Second, there are a lot of DeeJays in this world. And therefore there's a lot of competition. And competition means lower prices.

Let's assume you want to hire a live band for your wedding. Here are a few assumptions to keep in mind. The more popular a band is, the more likely it is to charge more. Also, more people in a band will increase the cost to hire it. Finally, if the band works with an agency, the band will add 5 to 20 percent onto your total cost.

Wedding bands that have been around for a while know how to negotiate with you for services. Bands that are just starting out in the business may not have a clue. If you can find a band that's just starting out and you trust the band to deliver, go for it. Of course, make sure you hear or see them play before you make a commitment.

A lot of bands will have two rate structures — one for pubic performances and another for private affairs. Some bands will adjust their price if they believe it will lead to future business. For example, they may be willing to lower their price if you have lots of folks at your reception who would be interested in hiring them at a future date.

Therefore, when the leader of a band negotiates rates with you, they want to know a few other things from you first before they quote you a price. When's the date of the performance?   Most likely they will charge more for weekends and holidays. They also want to know how much travel is involved and whether there are any complexities in setting up.

Musicians also decide on a rate based on how much they need the work, so visit their website and see if their calendar is typically filled. If not, you may get a break on cost. You may also bring down the price by offering the possibility of publicity for the band. Obviously, you'll have to be creative with weddings and receptions but you never know. Another factor the band may consider in lowering its price is whether the location is some really cool place to play. Is it on the beach? Or is it in a first-class hotel? Don't be afraid to negotiate a price. Simply start by saying you have a budget for the music. Bands always have a range of rates — a low and a high end — and they'll usually have some flexibility to give a little.

They may provide you with a price quote and tell you it's based on a similar gig they did in the past. Don't flinch, however. If it's too high, just say so. They may ask you again what you normally pay, but don't say anything. Let them provide you with a quote you can live with. You can always tell them you'll think about it and wait for an e-mail message from them that suggests a lower rate.

In the end, they may come down to your proposed rate or even something close, but they may want you to pay for expenses, such as mileage and meals. It's up to you. Remember, it's all about supply and demand. Most musicians are not making a full-time living out of playing. There are plenty of bands that just enjoy playing at any rate. And while it's important to avoid breaking your bank when hiring a musician for your wedding or reception, it's also important to remember that great music can make a significant difference on one of the most important days of your life. If you can afford that piano-playing doggy in the window and it makes you happy, then you know what to do.

16 - ETIQUETTE FOR WEDDING MUSICIANS

Playing music professionally – especially at a special event like a wedding – requires a bit more than simply sounding really great. Unfortunately, a great-sounding band that doesn't understand how to behave during a wedding reception can really be a downer.

I'm not a fan of too many rules and regulations when I play music, but there must be some set of principles by which musicians will adhere to when performing. Luckily, these principles have been created and agreed-upon by members of the Wedding Musician Association (.org), a non-profit organization comprised of professional musicians committed to providing the best possible music and service to their clients. Admittedly, the principles border on being preachy (my one criticism), but they do make sense. These principles are listed below (in bold) along with my comments:

Never discriminate on the basis of race, religion, sexual orientation, cultural traditions or age. Obviously, this is a no-brainer but you'd be surprised at how many times musicians will turn down a gig because of these factors. When you are a business, you should not discriminate against your customers.

Listen to your client and try to understand their vision for success. Wedding vendors, and not just musicians, can smell when a bride and groom don't know what they're doing and tend to take over. Sometimes it's challenging to understand what the bride and groom want, but we've got to try and find out. Instead of jumping in with our own ideas, it's better to wait and let the couple find their own basic vision, first. Then we can add our own suggestions.

Be a supportive consultant and service provider to wedding planners. Musicians will often keep them themselves isolated from the planning process of a wedding. In fact, many musicians have left the wedding business because there are too many questions and phone calls from the bride, groom, and wedding planner. The wedding planners are in charge and so I always make sure I understand their needs as well. Granted, it's not always possible to make everyone happy, but we can try.

Pay attention to all the details. It's why I always ask so many questions of my clients ahead of time.

Make certain to ensure the safety of your client and guests. Yes, I've had the father of the bride trip and fall on a power cord. It wasn't a pretty picture and I learned the hard way to take all the necessary precautions. A lot could happen and musicians should be prepared for anything. Incidentally, not all musicians have liability insurance, and they should.

Offer opportunities for guests to become involved whenever possible. For some reason, especially during wedding receptions, guests like to become involved with the music. Either they want to make requests, or ask you to turn the sound volume up or down, or they want to sing along, or play the tambourine. What's important to remember is that musicians do have a relationship with their audiences. They are not simply playing music behind a curtain.

Whenever possible, provide a guest microphone. Wedding musicians should always have an accessible microphone for people to make announcements, toasts, etc. Musicians should avoid using their own microphone for such purposes.

Know the management rules and regulations of the venue in advance. If I have never played at a particular hotel, I'll make certain I understand the hotel's policies for accommodating musicians and their equipment.

Be prepared for specialized electrical requirements and bring backup equipment. It's really quite frightening to be at an event when some vital piece of equipment doesn't work, so I bring backup equipment just in case.

Never take more time for a break than your performance agreement allows, and always let your client know where you will be located. For some reason, people like to make announcements when the band is on a break. Nothing is more frustrating to a client than not knowing how to find any members of the band. Also, if it's appropriate, the musician should play some pre-recorded break music while gone.

Be familiar with and respect the culture and tradition of your client. Not all wedding ceremonies, receptions, or people are the same.

Fully know all necessary protocol for weddings & receptions. This should be the number-one principle. Musicians are often part of a time-honored tradition, so they should be very familiar with the protocol and all of the procedures and their variations.

Always charge fairly for your services and make certain your client understands and agrees fully with any performance contract. Integrity, honesty, and good communications are important factors when working with clients. There should be no room for deception by any musician. Expectations should always be clear for both parties.

Never drink alcohol or smoke tobacco in or near the venue. Don't even do it on a break unless you are located where no one can see you.

Never display a "tip jar," merchandise or business cards. Tacky practice – especially at weddings. Musicians should always have their business cards available, just not on display.

Wear suitable clothing as advised by your client. Hello? It's called getting with the program. Not all musicians ask in advance about dress, however.

Never setup or pack your equipment while guests are still located in the performance area. It happens all the time. The musical clock stops at midnight, but the party keeps going and the band needs to pack up and get out. It's not always possible to avoid packing while the party is still going on, but musicians should try and wait. If it's not possible, confer with the client.

Avoid being a "celebrity" during your performance and remember: It's not about YOU. Musicians, me included, have egos. And sometimes when we have the microphone it's easy to believe we're the star of the show. And, frankly, when I'm playing at a club or theater, hopefully I am the star of the show. Weddings, however, are a very different story. Musicians at weddings are like good meeting facilitators. They keep things moving, but they don't control the meeting.

18 - ROLE OF MASTER OF CEREMONIES

The role of the Master of Ceremonies (MC) is to make certain all events at the reception move in an orderly and entertaining way. From the very first guests to the exit of the bride and groom, the MC should serve as the event organizer without being the "star" of the show. A great MC knows how to keep everything moving without dominating. If possible, having the lead singer of the band serve as the MC can be a real benefit because music often punctuates and underscores many of the key events during the reception. Find someone who can orchestrate the reception and play great music at the same time. You'll not only save money, but also be relieved of making certain everything runs smoothly and you'll have more time to enjoy the festivities.

Your MC should:

- ○ Check all of the audio equipment, microphones and sound levels of the music long before the guests arrive.

- ○ Introduce members of the wedding party as they arrive to the reception.

- ○ Recommend to guests they make take photographs of the bridal party.

- ○ Direct special guests to their reserved tables.

- Welcome guests on behalf of the wedding couple and announce dinner.

- Introduce members of the head table to the guests after dinner.

- Introduce the best man and bridesmaid to give toasts to bride & groom.

- Introduce anybody else to deliver to toasts, such as groom's parents.

- Introduce out-of-town guests, or acknowledgement of others.

- Introduce whoever will say grace.

- Announce the availability of drinks.

- Announce the logistics associated with dinner.

- Announce the cutting of the cake by the bride and groom.

- Announce the start of dancing and the bride and groom's first dance.

- Announce the father and daughter dance, and then the mother and son dance.

- Announce all others to come to the dance floor.

- Announce the tossing of the bridal bouquet.

- Announce the removal and throwing of the garter.

- Announce the last dance of the bride and groom.

- Announce the departure of the bride and groom.

- Make any additional announcements and keep the party going until the end.

20 - SELECTING OTHER WEDDING VENDORS

Always be careful when selecting the companies or individuals who will provide you with products or services for your wedding and reception. Unfortunately, vendors can say almost anything in their promotional materials. They can even make up testimonials from past clients or say things about themselves which are untrue. However, if your vendor already has a good reputation for providing products or services, you may not have to do much research. So, how do you trust vendors you don't know to deliver exactly what you require at a reasonable price? Here are eight general guidelines:

1. Read all of the promotional material very carefully. If something doesn't look right, question it. Not every vendor can produce the perfect website, but vendors should take pride in displaying and describing what they have to offer. Usually, many successful businesses have the most user-friendly and informative web sites.

2. Don't just believe the testimonials you read on the vendor's web site, but try to contact some of the people who have actually worked with the vendor. If your vendor cannot provide the name and phone number of a customer, walk away.

3. Review samples of the product. If it's a musician, either see the band perform in person or review a video of the band playing live. And make sure you hear more than one or two songs. For your caterer, taste the food. If possible, actually look at the table settings.

4. Make sure your vendor is a member of an organization -- like the Better Business Bureau -- or has a statement of quality assurance or performance standards. By the way, vendors who are also members of professional associations with standards may or may not practice those standards.

5. How long has the vendor been in business? Brand new vendors can very often provide good products or services at very reasonable prices, but be careful and always trust your instinct.

6. Meet your vendor in person, if possible. You don't have to meet every single person who will contribute to your wedding, but you should meet with those people who could be instrumental in making your event successful or not so successful.

7. Shop around to compare similar vendors. Review the promotions, prices and promises of several businesses offering similar products. By reviewing a number of vendors, you can make a more informed decision.

8. Test the vendor's commitment to customer service. How focused are they on our needs? Do they listen well? Do they return phone calls or e-mail messages, promptly? Again, use your instinct to understand their level of commitment to serving your needs.

COUNTDOWN CHECKLIST TO WEDDING DAY - 21

6 Months (Before Wedding)

- First and foremost, you should talk to each other about the vision you both share for the kind of wedding ceremony and celebration you desire. Do you want the traditional ceremony or something a little more non-traditional? Think about all possibilities and don't let anyone else force you into making a decision you don't really want to make.

- Decide on theme or color scheme for your wedding and reception. Start exploring all the steps you must take and all of the protocols for getting married before you make any financial decisions. Pick up a few wedding magazines and visit some of the wedding-related web sites on the Internet.

- Start keeping a notebook filled with your ideas, names and numbers, prices, and any other information you learn so you'll have all the details about your wedding in one place. You may also wish to use the notebook as a diary to record your thoughts and feelings as you move closer to your wedding day.

- Pick a date for your wedding and make sure the day is based upon your own preference, as well as the availability of venues and of guests.

- Consider appointing someone -- like a professional wedding planner, family member or friend -- to plan your wedding. Don't try to do it alone!

- Start working on a realistic budget and make sure you decide who will pay for what.

- More and more couples create their own website and a blog to post their thoughts, photographs, and videos for their families and friends to see. Some free services and websites offer an opportunity to send e-invitations to guests, as well.

- Now's the time to identify the members of your wedding party. Remember that most members, if not all, will play key roles in the wedding and can help you with the actual planning. Your wedding party should be comprised of close friends and family members who you trust to help. Once selected, think about inviting them to a planning meeting so they feel more like a part of everything.

22 - COUNTDOWN CHECKLIST TO WEDDING DAY

o   Send a written announcement and photograph of your engagement to your newspaper.

o   Identify and meet with the clergy or officiant who you want to lead your wedding ceremony. And don't forget to bring a list of questions to the meeting.

o   Pick out your invitations and stationery and make certain it fits with the theme and colors you selected for your wedding.

o   Decide on the type of formal or informal clothes you and the members of your wedding party will wear during the ceremony, and order them now.

o   You should start reviewing venues for the rehearsal dinner, wedding ceremony and reception.

o   Begin reviewing caterers, bakeries, limousine companies, travel agencies, photographers, videographers, florists and musicians.

3 – 6 Months (BW)

o   Start getting written agreements with important vendors, such as caterers, bakeries, limousine companies, travel agencies, photographers, videographers, florists and musicians.

o   Choose your registry services and begin selecting the gifts you would like to receive from your friends and family.

o   Schedule a date for the fitting of your clothes for you and members of your wedding party.

o   Finalize the site for the ceremony, rehearsal dinner and wedding reception.

o   Order your wedding rings, together.

o   Make final plans for the honeymoon, such as airline, hotel, and car rental. Don't forget to get your passports, if needed.

o   Decide on the type of musician or music you'll need, such as live band, solo musician, or DeeJay.

- Now it's time to select your musician for the rehearsal reception, wedding ceremony and reception. Make sure you obtain an agreement in writing, such as an e-mail confirmation.

- Decide if you want a Master of Ceremonies (MC) for the wedding reception. Very often, the live band or DeeJay you select can also serve as the MC.

- Secure a contract with the transportation company for a limousine for the bride and groom.

- Finalize plans for your rehearsal and associated dinner and reception.

- Make certain you now completely understand how to obtain a marriage license.

- Select the flowers and arrangements for all the bouquets, corsages, and decorations.

- Find a professional studio photographer and have your portrait taken.

- Make an appointment to get your hair and makeup done in preparation for the portrait.

2 to 3 Months (BW)

- The guest list should be completed and you should start sending out invitations.

- Finalize everything with the catering, bakery, and floral vendors. Make certain you can taste the samples of food, but don't eat the flowers.

- Locate a hotel to reserve rooms for your out-of-town guests and family members. Think about something your out of-town guests can do like an organized tour of the area or going to a show.

- Identify what you'll need to rent, like tents, chairs, silverware, decorations, and lighting.

- Consider producing a video or slide presentation of old photographs of the bride and groom which can be shown continuously during the reception. You can also upload the video or photographs to your website.

- Design and order any special banners or very large photographs to be displayed during the wedding reception.

24 - COUNTDOWN TO WEDDING DAY (CONT'D)

- Order any special clothing or lingerie required for the wedding rehearsal, ceremony, reception or honeymoon.

3 to 8 Weeks (BW)

- Start considering whether you want to write your own vows and what readings you may want to hear during your ceremony. You should start writing the vows now and complete them before you meet with the clergy or officiant again.

- Obtain your official guest book for the wedding and reception.

- Select and order any special gifts from the bride and groom to be given to members of the wedding party and or to any other special guests.

- By now, everyone in the wedding party should have the fittings for their clothing completed.

- If possible, the bride's maid and the groom's best man should each plan a separate party for members of the wedding party who are associated with either the bride or the groom.

- Make certain all logistics are finalized with the clergy or officiant.

- Complete and submit all forms for changing names, social security, insurance, driver's licenses, and addresses.

- Send your written wedding announcement and a photograph to your newspaper, any wedding websites and all other wedding publications.

- Confirm the rehearsal and reservations for the rehearsal dinner and reception.

- Contact every vendor with whom you've contracted and confirm what they are providing.

- Get the wedding rings and make sure they're tucked safely away.

- Go get the marriage license, together.

- Confirm all your reservations for the honeymoon.

- Speak with your videographers, photographers and musicians to confirm they know your precise expectations.

- Meet with the MC to develop a script for all events of the wedding reception. Make sure your MC knows the tone for the reception and the type of humor that may be appropriate. Also, provide the MC with a complete phonetic list of names to be announced.

- Send the formal invitation for the rehearsal and rehearsal dinner to all members of your wedding party and any special guests.

- Let someone know how you'd like your limousine decorated and stocked with refreshments.

1 Week (BW)

- Call all of the guests who have not responded to the invitation.

- Plan all the seating arrangements for the wedding reception

- Write and print a welcome note and agenda for the wedding ceremony and the reception.

- Prepare and print the place cards for the reception.

- Speak with whomever will toast the bride and groom to express your personal desire for the tone of the toast.

- Go down the list and make sure all of the details are in order, such as cake knife, toasting glasses, ring pillow, gifts for guests, cameras for guests, etc.

- Finalize all travel and reservation details for your honeymoon. Oh, and now is a good time to pack your suitcases before things become too hectic.

- Make sure the limousine driver knows what to do.

- If possible, try treating yourself to some special time alone before the big day. For example, spend a weekend at a resort or spa, or just relax somewhere in the country.

26 - COUNTDOWN TO WEDDING DAY (CONT'D)

1 Day (BW)

o   Pick up all the rented clothing and deliver it to the members of your wedding party.

o   Attend the wedding rehearsal and dinner, and don't drink too much and go to bed early.

Wedding Day

o   Thanks to your great preparation and delegation of responsibilities, everything goes smoothly and your wedding day becomes one of the greatest memories of your lives.

Have you considered original music composed especially for your wedding and for the soundtrack for your wedding video?

Excerpt from "The Prophet"
by Khalil Gabran

You were born together, and together you shall be forevermore. You shall be together when the white wings of death scatter your days. Ay, you shall be together even in the silent memory of God. But let there be spaces in your togetherness, And let the winds of heavens dance between you.

Love one another, but make not a bond of love: Let it rather be a moving sea between the shores of your souls. Fill each other's cup but drink not from one cup. Give one another of your bread but eat not from the same loaf. Sing and dance together and be joyous, but let each one of you be alone, Even as the strings of a lute are alone though they quiver with the same music.

Give your hearts, but not into each other's keeping. For only the hand of Life can contain your hearts. And stand together yet not too near together: For the pillars of the temple stand apart, And the oak tree and the cypress grow not in each other's shadow.

Excerpt from "The Prophet"
by Kahil Gibran

Love has no other desire but to fulfill itself. But if you love and must needs have desires, let these be your desires: To melt and be like a running brook that sings its melody to the night. To know the pain of too much tenderness. To be wounded by your own understanding of love; And to bleed willingly and joyfully.

To wake at dawn with a winged heart and give thanks for another day of loving; To rest at the noon hour and meditate love's ecstasy; To return home at eventide with gratitude; And then to sleep with a prayer for the beloved in your heart and a song of praise on your lips.

"My Luve" by Robert Burns

O my luve is like a red, red rose,
That's newly sprung in June:
O my luve is like the melodie,
That`s sweetly played in tune.
As fair art thou, my bonie lass,
So deep in luve am I;
And I will luve thee still, my dear,
Till a` the seas gang dry.
Till a` the seas gang dry, my dear,
And the rocks melt wi` the sun;
And I will luve thee still my dear,
While the sands o` life shall run.
And fare thee weel, my only luve!
And fare thee weel a while!
And I will come again, my luve,
Tho` it were ten thousand mile

From the "Song of Solomon"
- King James Bible version

My beloved spake, and said unto me, Rise up, my love, my fair one, and come away. For lo, the winter is past, the rain is over, and gone.

The flowers appear on the earth, the time of the singing of birds is come, and the voice of the turtle is heard in the land. The fig tree putteth forth her green figs, and the vines with the tender grape give a good smell. Arise, my love, my fair one,

"The Passionate Shepherd to His Love" by Christopher Marlowe

Come live with me, and be my love,
And we will all the pleasures prove
That valleys, groves, hills and fields,
Woods, or steepy mountain yields.

And we will sit upon the rocks,
Seeing the shepherds feed their flocks
By shallow rivers, to whose falls
Melodious birds sing madrigals.

And I will make thee beds of roses,
And a thousand fragrant posies,
A cap of flowers, and a kirtle,
Embroidered all with leaves of myrtle.

A gown made of the finest wool
Which from our pretty lambs we pull,
Fair lined slippers for the cold,
With buckles of the purest gold.

A belt of straw and ivy buds,
With coral clasps and amber studs,
And if these pleasures may thee move,
Come live with me, and be my love.

The shepherds' swains shall dance and
sing, for thy delight each May-morning;
If these delights thy mind may move,
Then live with me, and be my love.

**"Wedding Prayer"
by Robert Lewis Stevenson**

Lord, behold our family here assembled.
We thank you for this place in which we
dwell, for the love that unites us,
for the peace accorded us this day,
for the hope with which we expect the
morrow, for the health, the work, the food,
and the bright skies that make our lives
delightful; for our friends in all parts of the
earth. Amen

**"How Do I Love Thee?"
by Elizabeth Barrett Browning**

How do I love thee? Let me count the
ways. I love thee to the depth and
breadth and height my soul can reach,
when feeling out of sight for the ends of
being and ideal Grace.

I love thee to the level of everyday's
most quiet need, by sun and candle-light.

I love thee freely, as men strive for Right;
I love thee purely, as they turn from
Praise. I love thee with a passion put to
use in my old griefs, and with my
childhood's faith.

I love thee with a love I seemed to lose
with my lost saints, --- I love thee with the
breath, smiles, tears, of all my life! --- and,
if God choose, I shall but love thee better
after death.

"She Walks in Beauty" by Lord Byron

She walks in beauty, like the night
Of cloudless climes and starry skies;
And all that's best of dark and bright
Meet in her aspect and her eyes:
Thus mellow'd to that tender light
Which heaven to gaudy day denies.

One shade the more, one ray the less,
Had half impair'd the nameless grace
(continued on next page)

Which waves in every raven tress,
…Or softly lightens o'er her face;
Where thoughts serenely sweet express
How pure, how dear their dwelling-place.

And on that cheek, and o'er that brow,
So soft, so calm, yet eloquent,
The smiles that win, the tints that glow,
But tell of days in goodness spent,
A mind at peace with all below,
A heart whose love is innocent!

"Roads Go Ever Ever On"
by J.R.R Tolkien

Roads go ever ever on,
Over rock and under tree,
By caves where never sun has shone,
By streams that never find the sea;
Over snow by winter sown,
And through the merry flowers of June,
Over grass and over stone,
And under mountains in the moon.
Roads go ever ever on
Under cloud and under star,
Yet feet that wandering have gone
Turn at last to home afar.
Eyes that fire and sword have seen
And horror in the halls of stone
Look at last on meadows green
And trees and hills they long have known.

"To Be One With Each Other"
by George Eliot

What greater thing is there for two human
souls than to feel that they are joined
together to strengthen each other in all
labor, to minister to each other in all
sorrow, to share with each other in all
gladness, to be one with each other in the
silent unspoken memories?

"A White Rose" by JB O'Reilly

The red rose whispers of passion,
And the white rose breathes of love;
O, the red rose is a falcon,
And the white rose is a dove.
But I send you a cream-white rosebud
With a flush on its petal tips;
For the love that is purest and sweetest
Has a kiss of desire on the lips

"To My Dear and Loving Husband"
by Anne Bradstreet

If ever two were one, then surely we.
If ever man were lov'd by wife, then thee.
If ever wife was happy in a man, compare
with me, ye women, if you can.

I prize thy love more than whole Mines of
gold, or all the riches that the East doth
hold.

My love is such that Rivers cannot
quench, nor ought but love from thee give
recompense.

Thy love is such I can in no way repay;
The heavens reward thee manifold I pray.
Then while we live, in love lets so
persever, that when we live no more, we
may live ever.

"Love Is A Great Thing"
by Thomas à Kempis

Love is a great thing, yea, a great and
thorough good. By itself it makes that is
heavy light; and it bears evenly all that is
uneven.

It carries a burden which is no burden; it
(continued on next page)

…will not be kept back by anything low and mean; it desires to be free from all worldly affections, and not to be entangled by any outward prosperity, or by any adversity subdued.

Love feels no burden, thinks nothing of trouble, attempts what is above its strength, pleads no excuse of impossibility. It is therefore able to undertake all things, and it completes many things, and warrants them to take effect, where he who does not love would faint and lie down.   Though weary, it is not tired; though pressed it is not straitened; though alarmed, it is not confounded; but as a living flame it forces itself upwards and securely passes through all. Love is active and sincere, courageous, patient, faithful, prudent and manly.

"Hope is the Thing with Feathers" by Emily Dickenson

Hope is the thing with feathers
That perches in the soul,
And sings the tune without the words,
And never stops at all,

And sweetest in the gale is heard;
And sore must be the storm
That could abash the little bird
That kept so many warm.

I've heard it in the chilliest land,
And on the strangest sea;
Yet, never, in extremity
It asked a crumb of me.

Sonnet 116 by William Shakespeare

Let me not to the marriage of true minds
admit impediments. Love is not love
which alters when it alteration finds,
or bends with the remover to remove:
Oh, no! It is an ever-fixed mark.

That looks on tempests and is never
shaken; it is the star to every wandering
bark, whose worth's unknown, although
his height be taken.

Love's not Time's fool, though rosy lips
and cheeks within his bending sickle's
compass come; love alters not with his
brief hours and weeks, but bears it out
even to the edge of doom.

If this be error and upon me proved,
I never writ, nor no man ever loved.

Sonnet 18 by William Shakespeare

Shall I compare thee to a summer's day?
Thou art more lovely and more temperate: Rough winds do shake the darling buds of May, And summer's lease hath all too short a date: Sometime too hot the eye of heaven shines, And often is his gold complexion dimm'd; And every fair from fair sometime declines, By chance or nature's changing course untrimm'd; But thy eternal summer shall not fade Nor lose possession of that fair thou owest; Nor shall Death brag thou wander'st in his shade, When in eternal *(continued on next page)*

...lines to time thou growest: So long as men can breathe or eyes can see, So long lives this and this gives life to thee.

Excerpt from "Love's Labours Lost" by William Shakespeare

But love, first learned in a lady's eyes, Lives not alone immured in the brain; But, with the motion of all elements, Courses as swift as thought in every power, And gives to every power a double power, Above their functions and their offices. It adds a precious seeing to the eye; A lover's eyes will gaze an eagle blind; A lover's ear will hear the lowest sound, When the suspicious head of theft is stopp'd Love's feeling is more soft and sensible Than are the tender horns of cockl'd snails; Love's tongue proves dainty Bacchus gross in taste: For valour, is not Love a Hercules, Still climbing trees in the Hesperides? Subtle as Sphinx; as sweet and musical As bright Apollo's lute, strung with his hair: And when Love speaks, the voice of all the gods Makes heaven drowsy with the harmony Never durst poet touch a pen to write Until his ink were temper'd with Love's sighs; O, then his lines would ravish savage ears And plant in tyrants mild humility. From women's eyes this doctrine I derive: They sparkle still the right Promethean fire; They are the books, the arts, the academes, That show, contain and nourish all the world: Else none at all in ought proves excellent.

From "Hamlet" by William Shakespeare

Doubt thou the stars are fire;
Doubt that the sun doth move;
Doubt truth to be a liar;
But never doubt I love.

From "Goodridge Vs. Department of Health" by Massachusetts Supreme Court Chief Justice Margaret H. Marshall

Marriage is a vital social institution. The exclusive commitment of two individuals to each other nurtures love and mutual support; it brings stability to our society. For those who choose to marry, and for their children, marriage provides an abundance of legal, financial, and social benefits. In return it imposes weighty legal, financial, and social obligations....Without question, civil marriage enhances the "welfare of the community." It is a "social institution of the highest importance." ...Marriage also bestows enormous private and social advantages on those who choose to marry. Civil marriage is at once a deeply personal commitment to another human being and a highly public celebration of the ideals of mutuality, companionship, intimacy, fidelity, and family.... Because it fulfils yearnings for security, safe haven, and connection that express our common humanity, civil marriage is an esteemed institution, and the decision whether and whom to marry is among life's momentous acts of self-definition.

How do I love thee? Let me count the ways!

Excerpt from "The Master Speed"
by Robert Frost

Two such as you with such a master
speed Cannot be parted nor be swept
away From one another once you are
agreed That life is only life forevermore
Together wing to wing and oar to oar.

From Two Fragments by Sappho

Love holds me captive again and I
tremble with bittersweet longing
As a gale on the mountainside bends the
oak tree, I am rocked by my love

"Maud" by Lord Alfred Tennyson

There has fallen a splendid tear
From the passion-flower at the gate.
She is coming, my dove, my dear;
She is coming, my life, my fate;
The red rose cries, "She is near, she is
near;" And the white rose weeps, "She is
late;" The larkspur listens, "I hear, I hear;"
And the lily whispers, "I wait."

She is coming, my own, my sweet;
Were it ever so airy a tread,
My heart would hear her and beat,
Were it earth in an earthy bed;
My dust would hear her and beat,
Had I lain for a century dead,
Would start and tremble under her feet,
And blossom in purple and red.

"He Wishes For Cloths of Heaven"
by W B Yeats

Had I the heavens' embroidered cloths,
Enwrought with golden and silver light,
The blue and the dim and the dark cloths
Of night and light and the half-light,
I would spread the cloths under your feet:
But I, being poor, have only my dreams;
I have spread my dreams under your feet;
Tread softly because you tread on my
dreams.

"To a Stranger" by Walt Whitman

Passing stranger! you do not know how
longingly I look upon you; You must be he
I was seeking, or she I was seeking (it
comes to me, as of a dream). I have
somewhere surely lived a life of joy with
you. All is recalled as we flit by each
other, fluid, affectionate, chaste, matured;
You grew up with me, were a boy with
me, or a girl with me; I ate with you, and
slept with you--your body has become not
yours only, nor left my body mine only;
You give me the pleasure of your eyes,
face, flesh, as we pass--you take of my
beard, breast, hands in return; I am not to
speak to you--I am to think of you when I
sit alone, or wake at night lone; I am to
wait--I do not doubt I am to meet you
again; I am to see to it that I do not lose
you.

CONSIDER HAVING SOMEONE READ
THE LYRICS FROM ONE OF YOUR
FAVORITE LOVE SONGS.

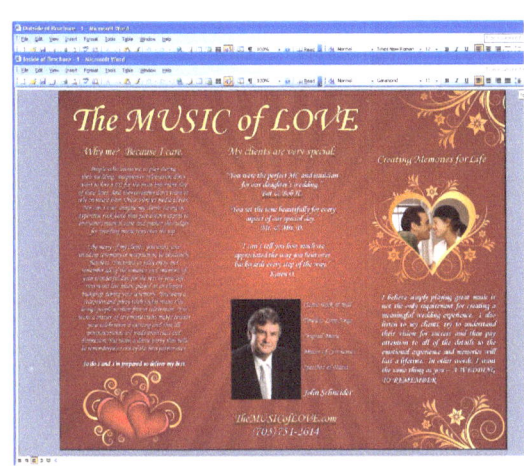

Wedding Web Sites
Bride.com
MyWedding.com
TheKnot.com
WeddingWire.com
WeddingVendors.com
MarthaStewartWeddings.com
PartyPop.com
ProjectWedding.com

Finding Wedding Musicians
Gigmaster.com
MDParty.com
WeddingMusicUSA.com

Original Wedding Music
OriginalMusicFactory.com

TheMUSICofLOVE.com

Bridal Shows
GreatBridalExpo.com
BridalShowcase.com

Music Associations
NameEntertainers.com
WeddingMusicianAssociation.org

Writing Services
WeddingWordsmith.com

New & Different Sites

Animoto.com automatically produces beautifully orchestrated, completely unique video pieces from your photos, video clips and music --fast, free and shockingly easy.

Arounder.com gives Honeymoon travelers a vivid sense of what a city has to offer: historical cathedrals and works of art, museums, local cafes and stores, breathtaking mountain-top views, quiet parks and gardens. The site contains a series of interesting panoramas providing a full immersive view of the cities. Navigation is easy with Google maps of the city and surrounding area, and links to local merchants with virtual tours of hotels, restaurants, spas and stores.

34 - GLOSSARY OF WEDDING TERMS

APERITIF: Very light, pre-dinner alcoholic beverage.

ASCOT TIE: Wide type of necktie usually for very formal daytime weddings.

BACKPIECE: Highly decorated comb (see comb) sitting on the back of a bride's head and used for attaching the veil.

BALLET: Also called a waltz, it's a veil length that drops below the bride's knees, but above her ankles.

BEST MAN: The best man usually keeps the bride's ring safe until the vows during the ceremony. He then hands the ring to the groom who puts it on his bride's finger. Other responsibilities include ding his own speech and announcing people to give their speeches at the reception. He also signs the marriage license and makes certain the groom gets to the wedding.

BIEDERMEIER: Tightly arranged cluster of flowers arranged in concentric circles and made in a circular shape, intricately-wired and arranged according to color.

BLUSHER: Short layer of veil worn over the face before the ceremony, then either flipped over the head or removed afterwards.

BOMBONIERE: Italian word which sometimes refers to wedding favors.

BOUTONIERRE: Single flower or bud worn in the lapel of the groom, best man, ushers and the male relatives of the bride and groom.

BOW TIE: Toe normally worn with a tuxedo and also called dickey bow.

BRIDAL OR BRIDE'S BOUQUET: Flowers given by the groom to his bride.

BRIDAL PROCESSION: Bride's entrance to the wedding ceremony, usually on her father's arm, with an accompanying entourage.

BRIDESMAIDS: Good friends of the bride who support her emotionally before and during her wedding. Bridesmaids normally pay for their own gowns, but the bride should advise them on required styles and colors.

CANDLE LIGHTERS: These are children who light candles at the altar when the bride's mother is seated.

CASCADE: Bouquet spilling downward into a sweeping collection of greens and flowers. (See Shower)

CASH BAR: Guests are charged for each drink they order as opposed to an open or hosted bar where guests are not charged because the host pays for everything.

CATHEDRAL: The most formal veil extending 3½ yards from the headpiece.

CEO/BEO: This stands for "Catering Event Order" and "Banquet Event Order". Caterers use a special document or spreadsheet for all the requirements of your function, such as the menu, overall table setup and staffing requirements.

CHAPEL: Formal veil extending to the floor to a length of 2½ yards from the headpiece.

CHEF: Executive cook in the kitchen. The sous chef is second-in-command in the kitchen.

CHIEF BRIDESMAID: (See Maid of Honor)

CLASSIC BOUQUET: This is the classic wedding bouquet which is a cluster of blooms, attached in a bouquet holder, wired, or hand-tied.

COMB: Another term for a haircomb which may be worn as the headpiece itself, or used in securing the veil.

COMPOSITE: Multiple flowers or petals wired together to resemble an oversized flower.

CORSAGE: Single flower bloom or small spray of blooms attached to lace and pinned on the front of a woman's dress or on her wrist. Orchids are a common flower used for corsages and are usually only worn by female relatives of the bride and groom.

SET: Tight-fitting top – which may be strapless or not -- with boning for support and lace-up or snap closures in the back.

CRESCENT: Half circle comprising large central flowers and smaller flowers on either side which could be made into a semi-crescent with flowers extending from one side.

CROWN: The bride may choose to wear a fully circular bead or gemstone adorned head piece that is larger than both a half crown and tiara.

CUMMERBUNDS: Pleated circles of fabric worn at the waist and without a vest. They are usually black, but may be any color.

DAIS: Podium or platform which is raised from the floor and where the bride and groom are seated during the reception. .

DIGESTIF: After-dinner drink such as cognac or Cointreau.

ELBOW: Length of veil which ends just above or below the elbow and comes in 6-, 8-or 10-button lengths.

EMBELLISHMENTS: Extra adornments on a bridal gown, such as embroidery, lace, glass or crystal beads, ribbons, bows, sequins, fringes, and others.

EMPIRE: Rounded bodice that ends just below the bust line.

ENGRAVING: Very formal method of printing which creates raised letters on the front of the invitation and an indentation on the back.

EURO TIE: Very often worn with a spread collar, this long tie is more formal than a regular necktie, but less formal than an ascot. (See Ascot)

FAVORS: Small inexpensive gifts given to all guests at a wedding to thank them for coming.

FIANCE: Title of the groom or husband-to-be between the engagement and the wedding.

FIANCEE: Title of the bride between her engagement to her betrothed and the wedding day.

FINGER TIP: One of the most popular lengths of veil which extends to the fingertips.

FINGERLESS: Glove with open finger holes.

FISH BOWL: Table centerpiece where flowers are together in a low, ornate bowl.

FLOWER GIRLS OR FLOWER CHILDREN: Small girls or children that pave the way down the aisle before the bride. Usually, they hold a pomander or scatter flower petals from a small basket. (See Pomander)

FLYAWAY: Informal style of veil reaching to the shoulders or a couple of inches below.

FOUNTAIN: This veil creates a visual effect around the face by gathering at the crown of the head.

FRENCH SERVICE: Style of service where food is prepared in large trays and portioned to patron's plates by the staff.

GARLANDS: Flower and/or leaves twirled into ropes that are hung from doorways, stairs and railings. A garland may also be worn by the bride as a headpiece. (See Wreath)

GAUNTLET: A long glove that does not cover the fingers and the end can come to a point over the hand.

GROOM'S CAKE: Smaller, second cake that may or may not be included in the wedding ceremony or served at the rehearsal dinner.

HALF CROWN: Ornate headpiece for the bride which lies between a crown and tiara in size and weight.

HALTER: Blouse-type top in which straps wrap around to tie or fasten behind the neck.

HEADBAND: Fabric band which holds back hair.

HONOR ATTENDANTS: The best man and the maid (or matron or man) of honor.

HORA: A dance at a Jewish wedding where the bride and groom are lifted while they sit on chairs.

HUPPAH: A flower canopy which is an integral part of Jewish weddings.

INTERLUDE: The interlude may be many different moments in the wedding ceremony, such as lighting the unity candle, memorial candle, or making the rose presentation. Interludes are moments of quiet reflection, and so the music should support this mood.

JACKET (TUXEDO, TUX): Classic tux jacket is worn at formal and semiformal events and comes in either a single-breasted (with a one- to four-button front) or a double-breasted (with a two- to six-button front).

JACKET (FULL DRESS, TAILS OR TAILCOAT): This jacket is cropped in front, with two tails in the back and a two- to six-button front and is worn at extremely formal evening weddings.

JACKET (CUTAWAY OR MORNING COAT): The cutaway coat is short in the front, long in the back, and tapers from the front waist button to a wide back tail. This style of jacket comes in black or gray, and is paired with matching striped trousers.

JACKET (STROLLER COAT): This suit jacket is cut like a tuxedo jacket, but in a semi-formal way, in black or dark gray and normally worn for weddings before the evening.

JULIET CAP: A close-fitting cap often decorated with precious stones and sometimes worn as a bride's headpiece.

KETUBAH: In Jewish weddings, this is the wedding contract between the bride and groom that is usually decorated, framed and later put on a wall in the couple's home.

KOUMBARO: Title of the best man in Eastern Orthodox Christian weddings. (See Crown)

LACE: A decorative mesh of interlaced threadwork which is plaited, knotted, looped and turned to make either simple or complicated patterns and raised work.

MAID OF HONOR: Also known as the chief bridesmaid, she is the last bridesmaid to walk down the aisle before the bride walks down. When the couple are exchanging wedding rings, it is her duty to hold the ring destined for the groom, and hand it to the bride at the right time. She will also hold onto the bouquets during the vows, and make certain the bride's dress is properly turned out.

MAN OF HONOR: Some brides have a male friend responsible for the duties normally assigned to the maid of honor.

MANTILLA: Circular Spanish-style lace or tulle attached with a comb or jeweled clips which the bride can wear around her head and shoulders.

MATRON OF HONOR: Proper title if the maid of honor is married.

MIDRIFF: This bodice fits tightly around the ribcage and reveals the stomach.

MISE EN PLACE: Refers to all the preparation for service, including table settings, beverage supplies, china, silverware, etc., or to the pre-cooked ingredients made by the chef before final cooking and presentation.

MOH: Stands for maid/man/matron of honor.

NOSEGAY: Small, round bouquet of densely packed round flowers, greenery, or herbs. (See Posies)

OFFICIANT: The cleric or secular official that carries out the ceremony. For non-religious weddings, the officiant may be a justice of the peace, magistrate or even the captain of a ship.

ONE MAN BAND: (Definition provided by Gigmasters.com) Gone are the days when the term "one man band" referred to someone who resembled Dick Van Dyke in the movie Mary Poppins. One man bands are extremely talented individuals that pack quite an entertainment punch! With numerous abilities, these performers are able to deliver a lot of value for the money. Within the GigMasters database, you'll find artists that play multiple musical instruments, those that play and sing, many who sing and DJ plus impersonators who also sing and dance. Because one man bands consist of one person and a few instruments, needed space is usually small but will typically require electricity. A great addition to weddings, anniversary parties, corporate events and more, the one man band is a fun way to deliver big entertainment even in small venues.

ONE-SHOULDER: (aka Asymmetrical) Having only one sleeve, or revealing one shoulder.

OPERA: A full, long glove that extends to the top or middle of the upper arm, most often with 12-16 buttons.

PAGES OR PAGE BOYS: These are small children (usually boys) who follow the bride down the aisle carrying some of her train. They can also be known as train bearers. (See Train)

PETIT FOURS: Bite sized, iced and elaborately decorated cakes, often served in addition to the wedding cake.

PILLARS: Supports, also known as columns, used to prop up the tiers of a multi-tiered wedding cake. They may be made from cardboard, plastic or wood.

PLATED SERVICE: Style of service where food is presented by the chef before the dishes are delivered to the tables.

POMANDER: Small, round cluster of blooms attached by a ribbon circle which are carried by flower girls in the bridal procession.

POSIES: This is a smaller version of a nosegay. Posies are the small and roundly shaped flower bouquets tightly packed with greenery and held together by a twine or sometimes a wire.

POSTLUDE: The musical postlude sets a pleasant atmosphere as guests are leaving and can last 10 to 30 minutes.

POUF: A gathering of netting secured with a headpiece or comb to give extra height to the veil.

PRELUDE: The purpose of the prelude music is to welcome guests as they are being seated before the ceremony. It also should give a cheerful yet subdued atmosphere, setting the stage for the solemnity of the event. The prelude generally begins 15 to 20 minutes before the ceremony starts. Because the prelude sets the tone for the rest of the ceremony, the music should be similar to the music used later in the ceremony.

PRESENTATION: A collection of long-stemmed flowers, tied together and held in one arm.

PRINCESS-LINE: This bodice has two seams that run over the bust line to the seam, elongating the chest and stomach.

PROCESSIONAL, BRIDE'S: Music played during the bride's entrance to the wedding ceremony. The traditional choice is Wagner's Bridal Chorus ("Here Comes the Bride"), but a number of classical selections can be played as well.

PROCESSIONAL, WEDDING PARTY'S: The wedding party's processional is the official beginning of the wedding ceremony. Therefore, the music should have be slow, elegant and dramatic as the bridesmaids and other members of the wedding party walk down the aisle. One favorite classical song is Canon in D.

RECESSIONAL: This selection of joyous music signals the officiant's pronouncement of husband and wife and the bridal couple walk back up the aisle. The most popular selection of music for the recessional is Mendelssohn's Wedding March, followed by Beethoven's Ode to Joy and Clarke's Trumpet Voluntary.

RING BEARER: Usually a child who walks down the aisle as part of the bridal procession carrying an ornamental cushion with the two replicas of the wedding rings on it.

SEMI-FORMAL: A less restrictive choice of clothing for semi-formal weddings.

SHORT: This is the end of the glove which is two inches above the wrist and may also be called a 'one-button' glove.

SHOWER: A spray of long-stemmed flowers which are often mixed with ivies which cascade downward as the bride holds it.

SNOOD: A knitted net worn by the bride at the back of her head to enclose her hair.

SOMMELIER: The wine expert at the location of the reception who has taken courses to earn the title. Others who have not take courses are known as wine stewards.

STROLLER COAT: A semiformal gray or black jacket resembling a tuxedo, but worn for daytime weddings.

SURPLICE: Fabric is crossed over the front or the back, giving a low neckline or low backline.

TASTING: The chef prepares a few samples of the menu for final approval before the wedding.

TIARA: A partial crown piece that affixes to the top of the head which may be worn as a headpiece or used to affix the veil.

TIE (BOW): The accessory for a formal tuxedo which forms a bow at the neck and may be worn in black or white. Groomsmen may wear different colored ties or choose the opposite or same as the groom.

TIE (NECKTIE): The traditional long tie for a formal or casual look.

TIE (ASCOT): A wide, formal tie that is usually patterned, folded over, and fastened with a stickpin or tie tack. This one is used for ultra-formal daytime weddings, paired with a cutaway coat and striped gray trousers.

TIE (BOLO): This western-type tie has a thick string tie fastened at the neck.

TIE (EURO): A combination of the ascot and necktie, this is a square-bottomed tie knotted in style at the neck and worn with a spread collar or wing collar.

TIERS: These are the layers of a wedding cake supported by pillars. (See Pillars)

TOSSING BOUQUET: This bouquet, which is a copy of the bride's bouquet, is thrown over the bride's shoulder towards bridesmaids and other single female guests after the wedding ceremony. Traditionally, whoever catches this bouquet will be the next to wed.

TRAIN: This is a long (or sometimes very long) extension to a wedding gown or other dress that trails behind along the floor.

TRAIN (CATHEDRAL): Extending some eight behind the gown, this train is used at very formal weddings.

TRAIN (CHAPEL): This is the most popular train for formal weddings which extends some three to four feet behind the bride's gown

TRAIN (COURT): The train extends one to two feet behind the bride's gown.

TRAIN (SWEEP): This is the shortest train which falls slightly behind the bride and just touches the floor.

TRAIN (WATTEAU): The train extends from its attachment at the shoulder blades and reaches just down to the bottom hem of the gown.

TRAIN BEARERS: (See Pages or Page Boys)

TULLE: This is a fine mesh used for bridal veils and wedding gowns.

TUSSY MUSSY: A posy carried in a small, metal vase.

TUX OR TUXEDO: This is a formal or semi-formal men's black evening jacket that may be either single-breasted (1-4 buttons) or double-breasted (2-6 buttons).

VOWS: During the wedding ceremony, the vows are exchanged between the bride and groom as their promises of loyalty, love, trust and support. Vows may be spoken as a statement or in response to the officiant's question.

VESTS (WAISTCOATS): A vest is worn under the jacket.

WAISTCOAT (VEST): For very formal evening weddings, men may wear a white tie and waistcoat.

WEDDING: Defined as the act of marrying, the ceremony or celebration of a marriage, the anniversary of a marriage (a silver wedding) or the act or an instance of joining closely (a wedding of ideas). There is no mention in the Bible of weddings as religious ceremonies because they were simply a legal and social occasion. Reportedly, there was a procession from the home of the veiled bride to the home of the groom which was followed by a banquet.

WEDDING MUSICIAN ASSOCIATION (WMA): Members of the Wedding Musician Association are professional musicians committed to provide the best possible music and service to their clients. All Members of the Association have agreed to comply with prescribed musical performance standards and ethical business practices.

WEDDING PLANNER: The job of the wedding planner is to coordinate all of the details involved in the process of two people being married, celebrating the marriage at a receptions and sometimes the travel arrangements for the honeymoon. They may order flowers, negotiate contracts with a photographer and videographer, arrange for musicians and book all other wedding vendors. They may also advise on color selections, ceremony and reception locations, and menu choices.

WING COLLAR: The most formal type of collar for shirts worn with a tuxedo.

WREATH: A circle of flowers an*d/or leaves often decorated with ribbons and bows. Wreaths are generally used as a centerpiece of a decorated area, or are seen above doorways. A small wreath may also be worn by the bride atop her head, if she so wishes. (See Garlands)

Your Musical Notes

All profit from the sale of this guide is donated directly to the Wedding Musician Association.

All the music of life seems to be like a bell that is ringing for me.

www.WeddingMusicianAssociation.org

www.ingramcontent.com/pod-product-compliance
Lightning Source LLC
Chambersburg PA
CBHW041517280526
45792CB00004B/1284